Oscarisms

Wisdom From a Seeing-Eye-Dog Dropout

First published by Busybird Publishing 2022

Copyright © 2022

Paperback ISBN: 978-1-925585-39-1

Busybird Publishing has asserted her right under the Copyright, Designs and Patents Act 1988 to be identified as the author of this work. The information in this book is based on the author's experiences and opinions. The publisher specifically disclaims responsibility for any adverse consequences, which may result from use of the information contained herein. Permission to use information has been sought by the author. Any breaches will be rectified in further editions of the book.

All rights reserved. No part of this publication may be reproduced, stored in or introduced into a retrieval system, or transmitted in any form, or by any means (electronic, mechanical, photocopying, recording or otherwise) without the prior written permission of the author. Any person who does any unauthorised act in relation to this publication may be liable to criminal prosecution and civil claims for damages. Enquiries should be made through the publisher.

Cover image: Kev Howlett

Cover design: Busybird Publishing

Layout and typesetting: Taylor Doyle

Images: Kev Howlett

Captions: Taylor Doyle, Sophie Breeze, Evie Thompson, Kit Russell, Kev Howlett, Blaise van Hecke, and Les Zig.

Busybird Publishing
2/118 Para Road
Montmorency, Victoria
Australia 3094
www.busybird.com.au

For Blaise ...

Welcome to my world of Oscarisms!

I've learned lots, experienced lots, and face every new day with a sense of adventure, love, and gratitude.

You can, too.

Let me be your guide!

Oscar

Look forward to the journey.

Don't get in over your head.

Sometimes you have to dig deep
to find the answer.

Daydreaming is fun.

There's nothing wrong with being a little shy ...

... but don't be afraid to stand out either.

Hard work doesn't always pay off
on the first try.

It's a long journey ahead, so ...

... just remember to look back every once in a while to see how far you've come!

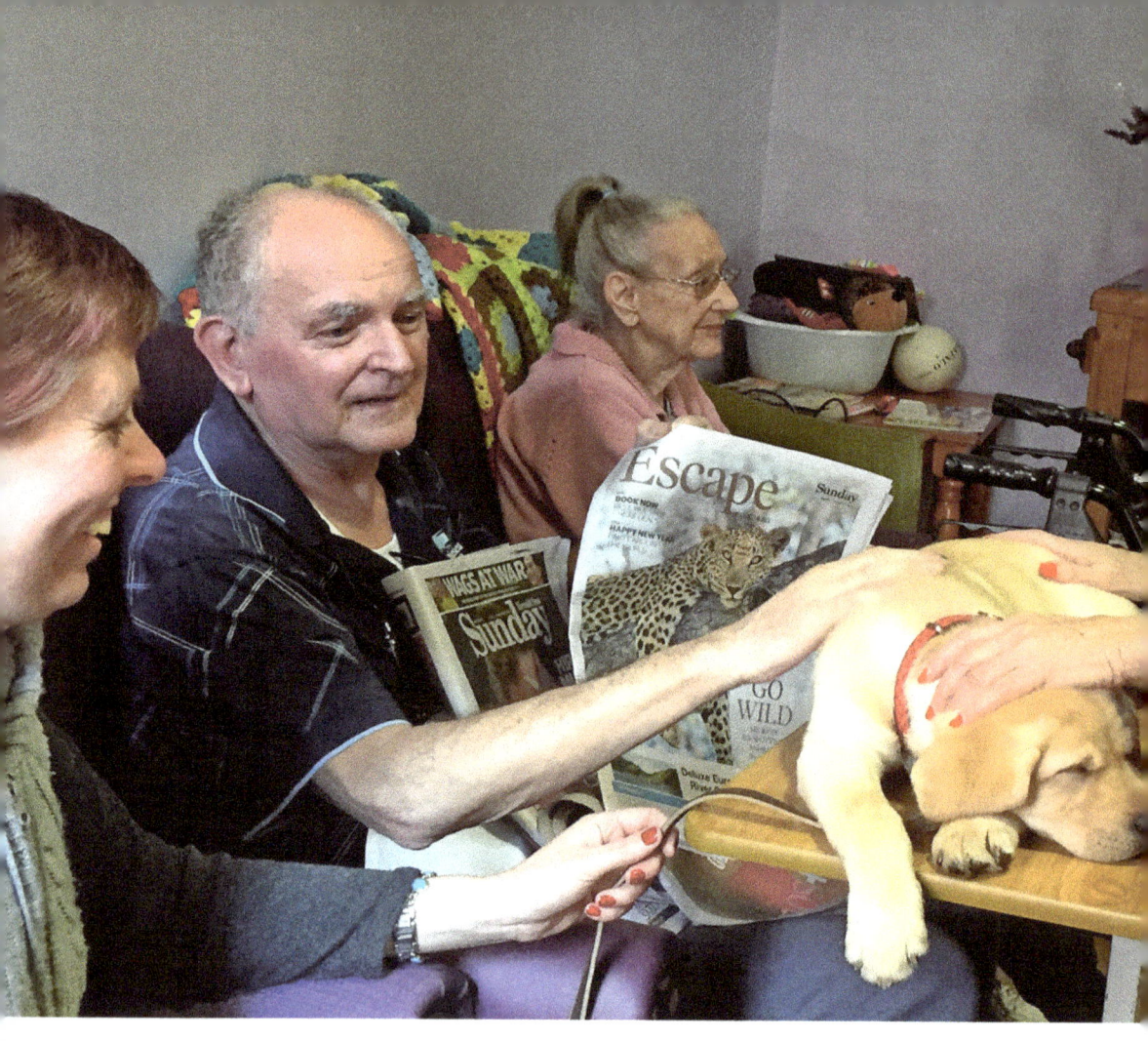

Spread your love and heal others.

You don't always have to put on a brave face.

Try and find some time to curl up
with a good book.

Scars are a badge of your strength.

Let yourself enjoy the simple pleasures in life.

Nurture the next generation with your wisdom and sensitivity.

Explore new experiences.

Chase a sunset.

Be patient. The tides will turn when they are ready.

Only you have the power to make your work fun.

If you truly, deeply want something, you will get it eventually.

Maybe if you just stare at it long enough …

... or try asking nicely.

It is the way you ask that makes all the difference.

Be silly when the moment seizes you.

Put your best foot forward.

Sometimes it's important to stop and reflect upon things.

Don't be afraid to get dirty.

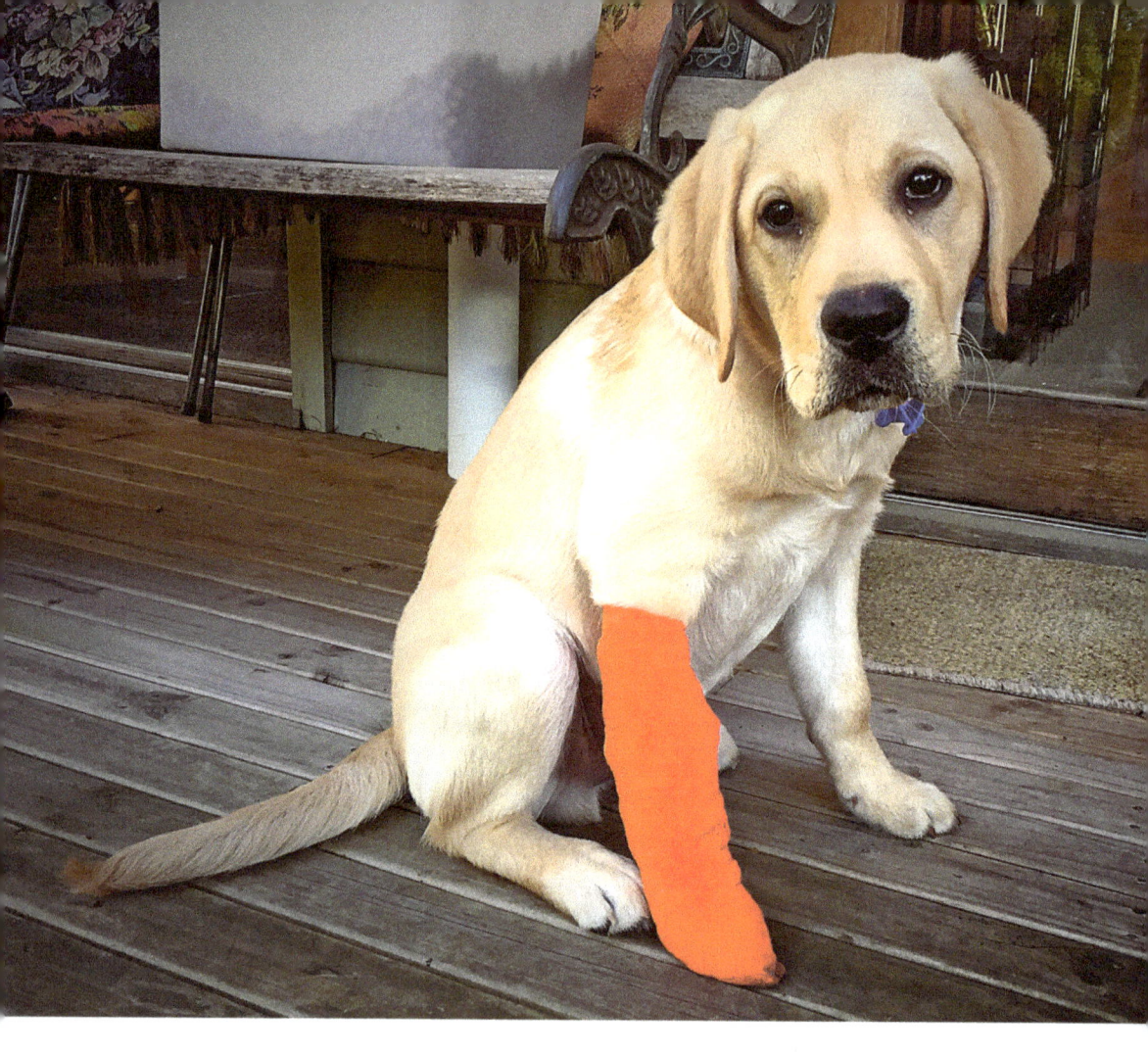

Your injuries do not define you.

Cast doubts aside and leap into the moment.

Sometimes all that's left to do is to say you're sorry.

Feel comfortable, wherever you are.

It's a big world, but you can make it your own.

When times get tough, release your inner warrior.

Tackle life's challenges with confidence.

If you're not confident, fake it until you make it.

Heed the important lessons.

Life is an adventure.

And tomorrow is a new day.

Always try to provide support for those who need it.

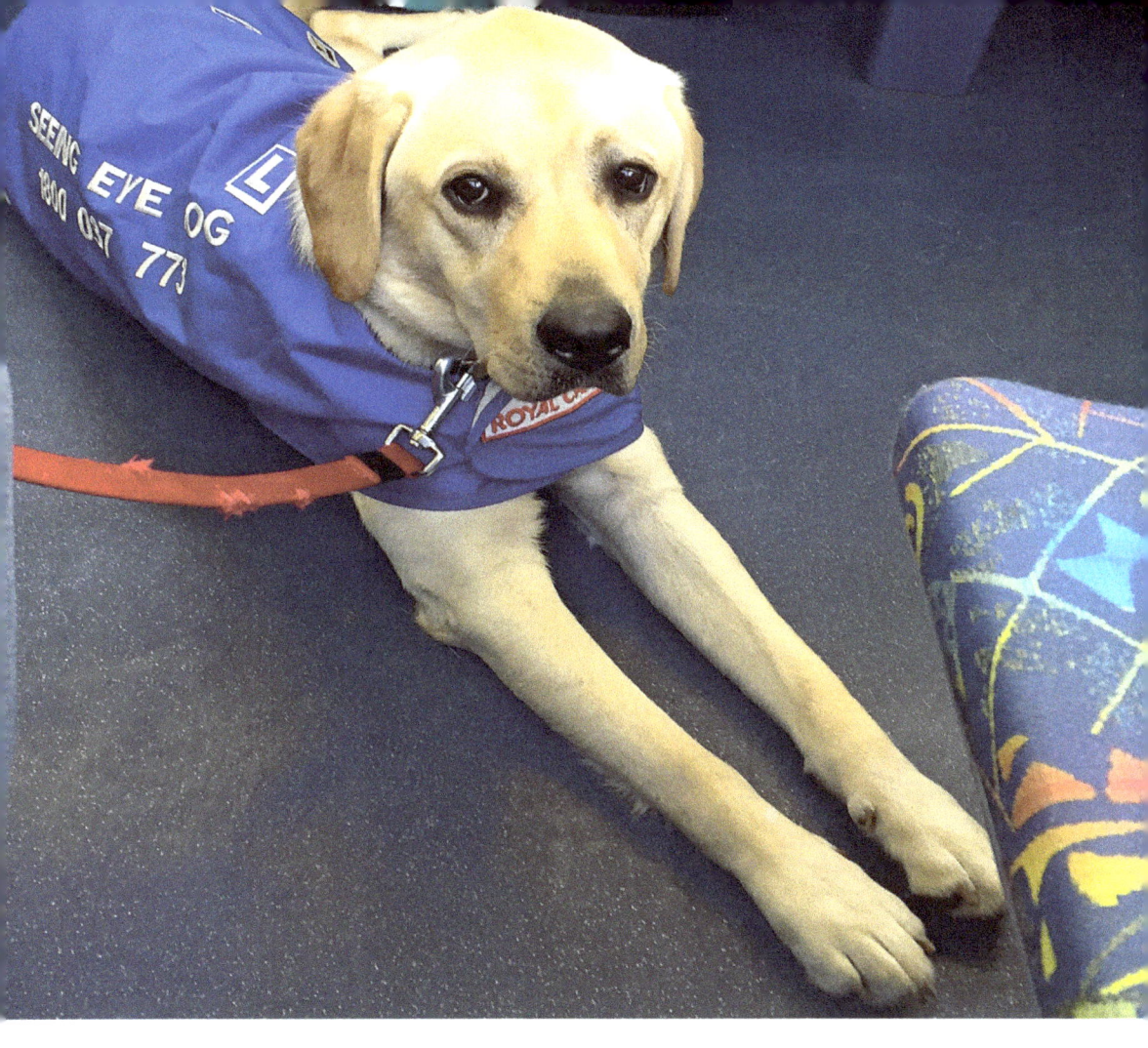

Don't be afraid to ask for guidance.

Eyes are the windows
to the soul.

Love knows no bounds.

Visualise what you want.

Trust in your friends.

There is no hole too deep to dig yourself out of.

It's okay to let yourself be lazy sometimes.

Listening is an important part of any relationship.

Do what you can to make your loved ones feel heard.

Everyone has a past, but it's how
you move forward in life that will define you.

Look to the future with purpose.

Be your most candid self.

Take stock of your surroundings and appreciate the beauty in where you are.

Never underestimate your capacity for adventure.

You are far stronger than you realise.

It's okay to be pensive sometimes.

But don't forget to smile once in a while!

At the end of a big day, don't be afraid to put your feet up.

Or, out.

Take pride in the places you live, love and learn.

Play hard ...

... dream hard.

Trust your instincts.

Always give your very best effort.

This big, beautiful world is a better place ...

... with you in it.

Tackle your ambitions head on.

Know when to call it a day.

Family isn't just about blood.

And friendship is forever.

busybird
publishing

Busybird Publishing is a boutique micropublisher based in the heart of Montmorency, Victoria.

We publish a handful of our own titles yearly, while also helping other authors get their stories out into the world. We make no claims on rights or royalties. They remain entirely yours.

We're a publisher run by creatives *for* creatives.

What's stopping you from telling your story?

To learn more about Busybird Publishing, check out our website:

www.busybird.com.au.

www.ingramcontent.com/pod-product-compliance
Lightning Source LLC
Chambersburg PA
CBHW051317110526
44590CB00031B/4384